CW00393194

So you <u>really</u> want to lea...

LATIN PREP

Workbook 1A and 1B
Answer Book

A. M. Wright

28/11/13

GALORE PARK

www.galorepark.co.uk

Published by Galore Park Publishing Ltd
19/21 Sayers Lane, Tenterden, Kent TN30 6BW

www.galorepark.co.uk

Text copyright © Anne Wright 2007

The right of Anne Wright to be identified as the author of this Work has been asserted by her in accordance with sections 77 and 78 of the Copyright, Designs and Patents Act 1988.

Typeset by Typetechnique, London W1

Printed by Charlesworth Press, Wakefield

ISBN: 978 1 905735 25 9

All rights reserved: no part of this publication may be reproduced, stored in a retrieval system, or transmitted in any form or by any means, electronic, mechanical, photocopying, recording or otherwise, without either the prior written permission of the copyright owner or a licence permitting restricted copying issued by the Copyright Licensing Agency, Saffron House, 6-10 Kirby Street, London EC1N 8TS.

First published 2007, reprinted 2008, 2010, 2011, 2012, 2013

Details of other Galore Park Publications are available at www.galorepark.co.uk

ISEB Revision Guides, publications and examination papers may also be obtained from Galore Park.

General guidelines for marking

- Latin to English sentences are given 1 mark per word (although occasionally 'non' or names attract no marks).

- English to Latin sentences are given 1 mark per correct word and another mark for putting the verb at the end.

- In comprehension questions, the answers show some extra information in brackets. It is not essential to provide this information to gain full marks.

- When translating from one language to another, there is often more than one correct way of reproducing the sense of the words. Sometimes, alternative answers have been indicated but, in general, assume that 'a' and 'the' can be supplied as necessary and that 'amo' can be translated as 'love' or 'like'. Also, note that the context may allow 'his', 'hers', 'ours' etc. to be used. For example, 'he takes his sword.'

- In the grammar exercises (the final exercise in each chapter), some explanation of grammatical points is given in italics in brackets – it is not necessary to write this extra detail to gain marks. The detail is provided to help pupils to understand the correct answer.

- Translation passages 1, 2 and 3 (Ex 1.11, 2.6 and 3.13) are marked at 1 mark per word, with no marks given for glossed words or names.

- Translation passage 4 (Ex 4.12) is marked at ½ mark for all words and an extra ½ mark for giving the correct verb tense.

- Translation passage 5 (Ex 5.12) is marked at ½ mark for every word.

- Translation passages 6 and 7 (Ex 6.17 and 7.8) are marked at ½ mark for all words and an extra ½ mark for giving the correct verb tense.

- Translation passage 8 is marked at 1 mark per word (except for glossed words) and an extra mark for giving the correct verb tense. The total mark is out of 45. Divide the total by 3 and multiply by 2 to give a mark out of 30.

- Translation passages 9 and 10 (Ex 9.7 and 10.2) are marked at ½ mark for all words and an extra ½ mark for giving the correct verb tense. No marks are given for glossed words.

Contents

Chapter 1 1

Chapter 2 4

Chapter 3 6

Chapter 4 10

Chapter 5 14

Chapter 6 18

Chapter 7 23

Chapter 8 26

Chapter 9 29

Chapter 10 32

Chapter 1

1.1

1.	plural	sailors
2.	singular	water
3.	singular	poet
4.	plural	farmers
5.	plural	women

1.2

1.	insulae	islands
2.	patriae	fatherlands
3.	deae	goddesses
4.	filiae	daughters
5.	puellae	girls

1.3

1.	femina	woman
2.	poeta	poet
3.	dea	goddess
4.	insula	island
5.	agricola	farmer

1.4

1.	you (s.) are
2.	they are
3.	you (pl.) are
4.	we are
5.	I am
6.	est
7.	sumus
8.	estis
9.	es
10.	est

1.5

1. they call
2. we work
3. you (s.) live/inhabit/dwell
4. you (pl.) fight
5. he/she/it hurries
6. aedificatis
7. ambulamus
8. amat
9. clamas
10. dant

1.6

1.	pugnamus	we fight
2.	cantat	he/she/it sings
3.	laudas	you (s.) praise
4.	aedificatis	you (pl.) build
5.	festino	I hurry

1.7

1.	you (pl.) walk	ambulo
2.	we shout	clamo
3.	they work	laboro
4.	you (s.) build	aedifico
5.	he/she/it asks	rogo

1.8

1. necamus
2. amatis
3. ambulant
4. aedifico
5. das

1.9

1.	amat	he/she/it loves
2.	estis	you (pl.) are
3.	rogamus	we ask
4.	sum	I am
5.	laudant	they praise

1.10

1. 'Greetings. Are you a poet?'
2. 'I am a sailor and I fight!'
3. Titus is a poet. He is singing.
4. Marcus.
5. Marcus is a farmer. He is lazy. 'non laborat' = 'he does not work'.
6. A farmer.

1.11

Sextus	'Are Gaius and Tiberius poets?'
Titus	'They fight and (they) shout. They are sailors.'
Julia and Laelia	'We are girls; we walk. And you? Are you girls?'
Cassia and Aurelia	'We are women; we sing.'
Aulus and Marcus	'Cassia and Aurelia sing.'
Titus	'They are women and (they) sing; you are farmers and you work.'

1.12

1. plural noun   nautae/feminae
   1st person singular verb   clamo/sum
   2nd person plural verb   pugnatis
   1st person plural verb   pugnamus/sumus
2. es
3. 3rd person singular
4. femina est
5. cantat
6. For emphasis – '*I* sing.'
7. Gaius poeta est. cantat.
8. agricolae laborant et (tu) pugnas.

Chapter 2

2.1

nom.	puella	puellae
voc.	puella	puellae
acc.	puellam	paellas

The nominative is used for the subject of the sentence.
The vocative is used for addressing someone or something.
The accusative is used for the object of the sentence.
The singular is used when one person or thing is involved.
The plural is used when more than one person or thing is involved.

2.2

1.	hastam	hastas	spears (object)
2.	ancilla	ancillae	O maidservants!
3.	poeta	poetae	poets (subject)
4.	deam	deas	goddesses (object)
5.	puella	puellae	girls (subject)

2.3

1.	nautae	nauta	O sailor!
2.	patrias	patriam	fatherland (object)
3.	feminae	femina	woman (subject)
4.	incolas	incolam	inhabitant (object)
5.	insulae	insula	O island!

2.4

1. The poets call the sailor.
2. The goddess praises the daughter.
3. The farmer calls the woman.
4. The farmers call the women.
5. The inhabitant loves/likes the islands.
6. The daughter does not kill the girl.
7. The sailor calls the woman.
8. The farmers love the maid-servants.
9. The farmers love the maid-servants.
10. The goddesses call the woman.
11. puella incolam amat.

12.   incola puellam amat.
13.   incolae puellas amant.
14.   nautam amamus.

2.5

1.   No. 'non festinat' = 'he does not hurry.'
2.   The girls. They call the farmer.
3.   'Why do you not hurry?'
4.   'You sing, but I carry water. I am working. I am not hurrying.'
5.   Yes – he is working (carrying water, not hurrying).

2.6

The inhabitants praise the girls but the farmer does not like the girls. He shouts, 'You sing but I work. I am a farmer and I do not like girls, I do not like daughters, I do not like women, but I love and praise the goddess.' (or 'I love the goddess and praise her.')

2.7

1.(a)   nominative – subject of the sentence
1.(b)   accusative – object of the sentence
2.(a)   2nd person singular
2.(b)   3rd person plural
3.   feminam
4.   amo
5.   They shout. An exclamation is when someone shouts out. The English word is derived from the Latin verb 'clamo' = 'I shout'.
6.   feminae agricolam vocant.
7.   agricola puellas non amat.

Chapter 3

3.1

1. puellarum
2. incolarum
3. aquae
4. poetarum
5. sagittae
6. agricolas
7. pecuniae
8. nautae
9. dea
10. sagittam

3.2

1. The girl loves the daughter of the sailor.
2. The girl carries the money of the queen.
3. The girls love the money of the queens.
4. The sailor carries the daughter of the woman.
5. The sailors love the daughters of the women.
6. puella pecuniam poetae portat.
7. puellae hastas poetarum portant.
8. nauta pecuniam deae non amat.
9. nautae pecuniam incolarum amant.
10. regina incolas insulae amat.

3.3

1. puellae
2. aquis
3. sagittae
4. nautis
5. insulis
6. dearum
7. irae
8. agricolam
9. sagittis
10. incolae

3.4

1. The girl gives water to the sailor.
2. The girl gives water to the sailors.
3. We are girls and we give water to the sailors.
4. The woman does not sing to the queen.
5. Why do the queens sing to the maid-servants and the sailors?
6. The inhabitant gives water to the woman.
7. nauta reginae cantat.
8. reginis pecuniam damus.
9. regina nautis cantat.
10. feminae nautis sagittas dant.

3.5

1. ira
2. agricolis
3. pecunia
4. reginis
5. ancillis
6. aquis
7. incola
8. poetae
9. nautae
10. patriarum

3.6

1. The sailor kills the poet with a spear.
2. The sailors kill the poet with spears.
3. The goddess kills the maid-servant with an arrow.
4. We do not kill the daughter with water.
5. The maid-servants kill the women with arrows and spears.
6. poeta puellam hasta necat.
7. poetae puellas hastis necant.
8. puellae poetas hasta necant.
9. ancilla incolam sagitta necat.
10. poetae sumus. sagittis non pugnamus.

3.7

1. servorum
2. muri
3. filiorum
4. librorum

5. dei
6. filium
7. servos
8. viri
9. equi
10. puerorum

3.8

1. The slave loves the horse of the master.
2. The slaves love the horses of the masters.
3. The friends of the boys do not build walls.
4. The boy calls the son of the master.
5. The slaves of the masters call the sons (or 'The slaves call the sons of the masters').
6. equi filios dominorum amant.
7. servus dominum equi non amat.
8. equus servum domini amat.
9. filius cibum dei portat.
10. filii cibum deorum portant.

3.9

1. amico
2. equis
3. puero
4. servis
5. dominis
6. filio
7. pueri
8. servum
9. deo
10. equi

3.10

1. The son gives the horse to the/his friend.
2. The teacher gives the books to the boys.
3. The boy gives the books to the teacher.
4. The boys give the food to the teachers.
5. The god gives the horse to the boy.
6. puer viro librum portat.
7. pueri magistro non cantant.
8. vir deo cantat.
9. viri dis et magistro cantant.
10. magister viris cibum dat.

3.11

1. deo
2. amicis
3. agro
4. cibis
5. muris
6. dominos
7. amice
8. deorum
9. cibum
10. equi

3.12

1. The son of the teacher and the friend of the son.
2. They shout and sing.
3. The teacher. At last.
4. 'Son, why are you not working?' (or 'Son, why do you not work?')
5. They are building walls.
6. She carries food and gives it to the women.

3.13

The son no longer sings but hurries. He carries water and gives it to the master. Soon a slave enters and shouts: 'Master, the inhabitants of the islands are here. They are killing the sailors with arrows.' The anger of the master is great. The master calls the men, women, boys and girls.

3.14

1.(a) patriae
1.(b) pugnamus
2.(a) ablative – they kill the men <u>with</u> the arrows
2.(b) dative – he gives money and horses <u>to</u> the men
3. subject – incolae   object – agros
4. domini virum
5. equine/equestrian – something to do with horses
6. domino pecuniam damus.
7. filiae amicorum cantant.

Chapter 4

4.1

1. periculi – of the danger
2. verba – the words (object)
3. oppido – with/by/from the town
4. vinis – to/for the wines
5. templum – O temple!

4.2

1. We stand on the wall!
2. The sailors fight in wars.
3. The farmers overcome the masters of the islands.
4. Son, why are you walking in the town? Why are you not working?
5. The teacher calls the slaves and asks about the maid-servants.
6. cum amicis ambulamus.
7. Sexte, cur ex oppido festinas?
8. in bello pugnamus.
9. cur in agris ambulatis?
10. poetae de dis insulae cantant.

4.3

1. The tired sailors hurry out of the deep water.
2. The bad boys do not work in the field but sing with the happy girls.
3. Many farmers are in the temple of the town.
4. You (s.) ask the good maid-servant, 'Who is fighting on the big island?'
5. We kill the bad inhabitants with a/the big/large spear but you (pl.) do not kill the good queen.
6. filia bona non laborat.
7. puellae fessae deam bonam laudant.
8. puerum multis sagittis necatis.
9. amici laeti non pugnant.
10. nautae fessi incolas superant.

4.4

1. I am good, but you (s.) are bad.
2. Where are the happy girls? The girls are walking out of the town.
3. Why is the boy tired? He is not working in the field.
4. The temples are high and big.
5. We give many books to the teacher.

6. puer bonus agricola est.
7. puella bona fessa est.
8. poetae boni libros magnos portant.
9. multae feminae in magno oppido sunt.
10. ubi est parvum templum deae? hic est!

4.5

Note that for all exercises using the imperfect, the verb can normally be translated as 'I was …ing' or 'I used to …'.

1. we were hurrying
2. you (s.) were entering
3. they were building
4. I was fighting
5. he/she/it was working
6. amabam
7. rogabant
8. portabamus
9. cantabat
10. aedificabas

4.6

1. clamabamus – we were shouting
2. aedificabatis – you (pl.) were building
3. laudabant – they were praising
4. rogabatis – you (pl.) were asking
5. necabamus – we were killing

4.7

1. intrabam – I was entering
2. amabas – you (s.) were loving
3. vocabat – he/she/it was calling
4. laborabam – I was working
5. festinabat – he/she/it was hurrying

4.8

1. The daughters were praising the goddesses but we were hurrying out of the town.
2. We were giving water and food to the tired horses.
3. The friends of the teacher were singing in the fields. We were hurrying out of the temple.
4. They were singing about horses and (about) great wars.

5. The women were calling the son and asking about the girls.
6. ex oppido festinabas.
7. servos malos vocabamus.
8. in templo habitabant.
9. domini fessi clamabant.
10. equo aquam dabatis.

4.9

1. we were
2. erant
3. estis
4. eratis
5. you (s.) are
6. sumus
7. I was
8. I am
9. you (s.) were
10. they were

4.10

1. We were not working in the fields because we were tired.
2. We carry the big books because the teacher is good.
3. The poet was singing about the queen and the queen was happy.
4. The son of the woman was big.
5. The food of the slaves was bad, but the food of the maid-servants is good.
6. puella parva erat.
7. laeti/laetae eratis. (laeti for masculine/laetae for feminine)
8. in templo deae eramus.
9. puero cibum dabas.
10. pueris libros damus.

4.11

1. The Greeks and Achilles.
2. He loved her.
3. Agamemnon was the king of the Greeks. He also loved her.
4. 'eam multis verbis laudabat.' = 'He was praising her with many words.'
5. At last Agamemnon called/was calling Achilles.
6. 'Where is she?'

4.12

Achilles was not happy. 'I love the maid-servant! The maid-servant is mine!' But Agamemnon shouts, 'I am the king and master. I want the maid-servant.' The anger of the man was great. However, he gives the maid-servant to the master. The Greeks were now in great danger because Achilles was not fighting. The inhabitants were hurrying from the walls of the town, overcoming the Greeks, and were killing many in the war.

4.13

1.(a)   vocative – the friend is being addressed
1.(b)   genitive – possession (the weapons belong to the friend)
1.(c)   ablative – the preposition ab takes the ablative
2.   3rd person singular, present tense
3.   sum
4.   amicos
5.   puellas
6.   festinatis
7.   sunt
8.   He kills Patroclus.
9.(a)   pugnas
9.(b)   cur/non/tandem
9.(c)   amicum/Patroclum/Hectorem
9.(d)   et/quod
10.   oppidum

Chapter 5

5.1

1. One woman was walking with four men.
2. Two girls stand on the walls of the big temple.
3. We were giving seven horses to the boy.
4. The farmer calls five slaves and asks, 'Where is the maid-servant?'
5. Three temples were in the town.
6. septem agricolas laudabamus.
7. tres pueri boni sunt.
8. sex poetae quattuor ancillas necabant.
9. duae feminae in oppido habitant.
10. novem templa aedificatis.

5.2

1. Six girls hurry to the temple.
2. The slaves were entering (into) the fields of the masters.
3. The friend was carrying food through the fields.
4. We were shouting and singing near the walls of the temple.
5. I was carrying the money of the queen across the fields.
6. per agros ambulabas.
7. deus belli in templo habitat.
8. magister in templum ambulat.
9. prope templa incolarum pugnabamus.
10. de quinque bellis cantabatis.

5.3

1. The Roman men have many slaves.
2. Why was the daughter giving food to the master?
3. The god has a big horse.
4. On the islands the inhabitants had much money.
5. The teacher has nine big books.

5.4

1. you (pl.) walked
2. you (s.) shouted
3. we called
4. he/she/it killed
5. I lived/inhabited/dwelt

6. amaverunt
7. dedimus (NB – watch the stem – do, dare, dedi, datum)
8. laboravit
9. pugnavisti
10. ambulaverunt

5.5

1. ambulavimus – we walked
2. amavistis – you (pl.) loved
3. portaverunt – they carried
4. necavistis – you (pl.) killed
5. dedimus – we gave

5.6

1. laudavi – I praised
2. vocavisti – you (s.) called
3. clamavit – he/she/it shouted
4. festinavit – he/she/it hurried
5. steti – I stood (NB – watch the stem – sto, stare, steti, statum)

5.7

1. We killed eight sailors with spears.
2. I praised the goddess but you (pl.) praised the gods.
3. The boys carried nine books through the fields.
4. The teacher gave much money to the queen. OR The teacher of the queen gave much money.
5. You (s.) stood in the temple and sang with five maid-servants.
6. in bello pugnavimus.
7. puellae Romanae in agros ambulaverunt.
8. in muro stetisti.
9. puerorum dominus septem feminas vocavit.
10. muros magni oppidi aedificavimus.

5.8

1. The beautiful women gave food to the sacred gods.
2. The master of the slave is bad and the slave was wretched.
3. The boys did not give books to the teacher. The teacher was angry.
4. Four Roman men were singing with the beautiful daughter.
5. Two maid-servants carried big spears through the fields.
6. e templo pulcho ambulas.

7. multas sagittas portavi.
8. deus in templum Romanum intravit.
9. cur servum miserum necavisti?
10. filio octo equi sunt.

5.9

1. fuerunt
2. fuisti
3. fuimus
4. fuistis
5. fuit
6. estis
7. erat
8. eram
9. sunt
10. fui

5.10

1. There was one beautiful woman.
2. The friend had nine arrows.
3. I killed many sailors in the sacred war with spears.
4. The boy worked in the field of the farmer and was tired.
5. You (pl.) fought with sacred arrows.
6. mali/malae fuimus! (mali for masculine, malae for feminine)
7. muri oppidorum pulchri non fuerunt.
8. filii reginae laeti fuerunt.
9. reginam de insulis pulchris rogabam.
10. servi virum Romanum hasta necaverunt.

5.11

1. The poet, with a big spear.
2. He called men and women. Three (beautiful) women and many men.
3. 'Were you (pl.) in the temple?'
4. She said Marcus was near the walls of the temple.
5. He said he was working near the walls.
6. Sulpicia.

5.12

Sulpicia shouted, 'I was praising the goddess! I was giving food to the goddess! But the two sons of the teacher were also in the temple!'

Quintus walked towards the boys. 'Wretched boys, why were you in the temple? Why did you kill the poet?'

'Near the temple is a wall. We were standing on the wall. However, a man walked towards the wall and, because the man was angry, we hurried into the temple.'

'Why was the man angry?'

'The temple is sacred and we were standing on a sacred wall.'

5.13

1.(a)   mali/iratus/bonum/magna/malus
1.(b)   estis
1.(c)   dixit/rogavit/clamavit/necavit
1.(d)   erat
2.(a)   vocative – addressing someone.
2.(b)   NB hasta is used three times in line 7. As the 2nd word it is ablative because someone killed the poet <u>with/by means of</u> a spear. As the 7th and 12th words it is ablative because the preposition de takes the ablative.
3.   subject – servus   object – poetam
4.   interrogate/interrogative/interrogation etc. rogo means 'I ask' and interrogate means to question someone closely.
5.   poetam portavimus.
6.   pueri puellas laudabant.

Chapter 6

6.1

1. he/she/it frightens/terrifies
2. you (pl.) warn/advise
3. you (s.) have
4. we remain/stay
5. I reply
6. respondemus
7. movet
8. iubes
9. terretis
10. monent

6.2

1. movemus   we move
2. timetis   you (pl.) fear
3. delent   they destroy
4. manetis   you (pl.) remain/stay
5. iubemus   we order

6.3

1. teneo   I hold
2. deles   you (s.) destroy
3. timet   he/she/it fears
4. moneo   I warn/advise
5. manet   he/she/it remains/stays

6.4

1. they were destroying
2. you (s.) were laughing
3. we were warning/advising
4. I was ordering
5. he/she/it was seeing
6. delebas
7. timebant
8. manebamus
9. ridebam
10. terrebat

6.5

1.	timebamus	we were fearing
2.	movebatis	you (pl.) were moving
3.	tenebant	they were holding
4.	delebatis	you (pl.) were destroying
5.	respondebamus	we were replying

6.6

1.	delebam	I was destroying
2.	habebas	you (s.) were having
3.	movebat	he/she/it was moving
4.	respondebas	you (s.) were replying
5.	monebam	I was warning/advising

6.7

1.	you (s.) saw/have seen
2.	you (pl.) (have) warned/advised
3.	he (has) frightened/terrified
4.	they (have) ordered
5.	I (have) replied
6.	delevit
7.	vidimus
8.	movistis
9.	timui
10.	monuisti

6.8

1.	mansimus	we (have) remained/stayed
2.	habuistis	you (pl.) (have) had
3.	terruerunt	they (have) frightened/terrified
4.	delevimus	we (have) destroyed
5.	riserunt	they (have) laughed

6.9

1.	movi	I (have) moved
2.	delevisti	you (s.) (have) destroyed
3.	tenuit	he/she/it (has) held
4.	respondisti	you (s.) (have) replied
5.	monui	I (have) warned/advised

6.10

1. Once the sailors destroyed the walls of the towns.
2. The teacher shouted, 'Why are you (pl.) sailing to the island?' The slaves replied, 'We fear the big waves.'
3. A big crowd was remaining in the town for a long time.
4. We called the slaves into the field. They did not hurry.
5. The teachers were warning the bad boys. However, the boys were not working.
6. servi cibum movebant.
7. puellam monui. non respondit.
8. in magnis agris ridebamus.
9. incolae mali muros oppidi delent.
10. agricolas et magistros timuimus.

6.11

1. Where did the sailors sail? Five were sailing towards us but three sailed to the islands.
2. Why does Decimus, the son of the teacher, not carry the book?
3. The men attacked the town; a crowd of inhabitants destroyed the walls of the town.
4. The bad horse frightened me but Julius, the friend of (the) beautiful girls, was not fearing/afraid of the horse.
5. We were sailing across the waves and now we attack the town.
6. navigavitne ad insulas?
7. ego pugnabam, sed tu me superavisti.
8. magistrum diu timebamus.
9. cur virum necavistis?
10. turba virum multis sagittis necavit.

6.12

1.	imperfect	we were departing
2.	perfect	he/she/it (has) led
3.	present	you (pl.) play
4.	imperfect	they were showing
5.	perfect	you (pl.) wrote/have written
6.	present	disceditis
7.	imperfect	ducebant
8.	perfect	scripsisti
9.	present	ducit
10.	perfect	legi

6.13

1.	imperfect	dicebamus	we were saying
2.	present	legitis	you (pl.) read/choose
3.	present	ducunt	they lead
4.	perfect	lusimus	we (have) played
5.	imperfect	legebatis	you (pl.) were reading/choosing

6.14

1.	perfect	rexit	he/she/it (has) ruled
2.	imperfect	scribebas	you (s.) were writing
3.	perfect	discessit	he/she/it (has) departed
4.	present	ostendis	you (s.) show
5.	imperfect	ludebat	he/she/it was playing

6.15

1. The teacher wrote many words in the books of the boys.
2. The farmer spoke about the fatherland and warned about danger.
3. The man was saying many things to Spurius, a/his good friend.
4. The farmer was asking, 'What did you say?' I said, 'Where is the water? Is it in the wine?'
5. The bad man frightened/terrified the inhabitants with spears and was ruling the inhabitants for a long time.
6. oppidum regebatis.
7. puellae laetae cum equis luserunt.
8. librum legisti? libros legi.
9. cur servos ad insulam duxistis?
10. feminae hastas ostendi.

6.16

1. Ulysses and his/the sailors.
2. (They departed) from the fatherland of the Trojans (and were hurrying) to/towards Greece.
3. 'diu' = 'for a long time.' (Accept 'tandem' = 'at last'.)
4. They were sailing across high seas, because of the anger of the gods.
5. (He saw) an island, at last.
6. He shouted, 'Sailors, here is an island.'

6.17

The tired men hurried onto the island and at last (they) saw an inhabitant. 'Who are you?' asked Ulysses. The inhabitant said to the men, 'I am Aeolus, the master of the winds.' Aeolus ruled the winds. He placed many winds in a sack and gave the sack to the sailors. One wind was not in the sack. At last Ulysses and the sailors sailed to the fatherland, but the sailors opened the sack.

6.18

1.(a)   ad patriam (the other prepositions in the passage – e/ex and a/ab – take the ablative case)
1.(b)   cur/iam/non
2.(a)   nominative – the subject of the sentence
2.(b)   vocative – they are being addressed
3.   3rd person singular, perfect tense, clamo
4.   subject – venti
        object – nos ('Now <u>the winds</u> drive <u>us</u> from our fatherland')
5.   superabant (change from the perfect to the imperfect of supero, superare, superavi, superatum –
        1st conjugation)
6.   miserable (misery, etc). If you are miserable then you are unhappy or wretched. The Latin adjective
        'miser' means 'unhappy' or 'wretched'. Both words are connected with degrees of unhappiness.
7.   agricolae puellas pulchras monebant.

Chapter 7

7.1

1. The fourth boy was walking with the fifth girl.
2. Where is the second horse, slave?
3. The women carry food to the seventh master.
4. We were near the fields and we stood on the third wall.
5. The tenth man was killing the sixth slave, but he greatly praised the third maid-servant.
6. cur sextus puer pugnavit?
7. cum quarto amico festinavimus.
8. tres poetae primum verbum cantaverunt.
9. nonus nauta trans undas altas navigat.
10. magister puellarum in secundum agrum intrat.

7.2

1.	perfect	they (have) slept
2.	imperfect	he/she/it was coming
3.	present	you (s.) sleep
4.	imperfect	we were hearing
5.	perfect	you (s.) (have) heard
6.	perfect	dormivistis
7.	present	audiunt
8.	present	dormimus
9.	perfect	venit
10.	imperfect	audiebant

7.3

1.	imperfect	audiebatis	you (pl.) were hearing
2.	present	dormiunt	they sleep
3.	perfect	venimus	we came/have come
4.	imperfect	veniebant	they were coming
5.	perfect	audivistis	you (pl.) (have) heard

7.4

1.	present	venis	you (s.) come
2.	perfect	venisti	you (s.) came/have come
3.	imperfect	dormiebas	you (s.) were sleeping
4.	perfect	audivi	I (have) heard
5.	present	dormit	he/she/it sleeps

7.5

1.   The angry teacher asked, 'Marcus, why were you sleeping and not working?'
2.   Three slaves came out of the town. They led the horses of the masters.
3.   We soon heard the words of the teacher and we hurried into the fields.
4.   The girls were standing in the fields but they were not hearing the boys.
        (OR were not listening to the boys.)
5.   'Why do you (s.) hurry towards the temple?' 'Because many poets come!'
6.   pueri laeti in agris dormiebant.
7.   amicus ancillae non venit.
8.   quod (viri) clamabant, viros audivimus.
9.   'cur dormis?' magister rogabat.
10.   iterum deam audivisti.

7.6

1.   The master ordered the slave to work.
2.   We order the sailors to sail to/towards the island.
3.   The queen at last decided to rule the/her fatherland.
4.   The crowd of men feared wars but decided to fight.
5.   You (pl.) decided/have decided to attack the town with the help of the gods; therefore the farmers and
        inhabitants hurry.
6.   per agros festinare constituo.
7.   filiam laudare constituit.
8.   tandem templum intrare constituimus.
9.   verba poetarum audire amo.
10.   filium non video. pugnare amat.

7.7

1.   The good poet of the goddesses.
2.   The Roman farmers; with spears and arrows.
3.   They attacked the second town.
4.   'We must (therefore) stand here and build walls.'
5.   Angry. (work out answer from information that 'The anger of the queen was great.')
6.   '(Men), you (pl.) must walk from the walls of the town.'

7.8

One man asked, 'Why?' The queen replied, 'You must lead the sailors across the high waves and near the town.' The queen warned the men about the great danger. At last, the men came out of the town. Soon the Romans were attacking the town again but, because they led the sailors, the men overcame the Romans. They were fighting bravely (and) for a long time; therefore the men killed many Romans.

7.9

1.(a) poetam
1.(b) erat (imperfect of the irregular verb 'sum – I am')
2.(a) dative – she gave money <u>to</u> the men
2.(b) accusative – the preposition 'in' meaning 'into' takes the accusative
3. subject – regina
    object – poetam ('because <u>the queen</u> did not listen to <u>the poet</u>')
4. 3rd person plural, perfect, laudo
5. fessae (change the masculine adjective to a feminine form)
6. dat (change the verb from the perfect to the present of do = 'I give' – remembering that the present conjugates 'do, das, dat' etc.)
7. 'he/she/it heard.' An audition is when people listen to someone performing for a place in an orchestra, play etc.
8. in bello pugnabamus. (in + acc. = into/onto; in + abl. = in/on. Use in + ablative here.)

Chapter 8

8.1

1.	imperfect	he/she/it was wanting/wishing/desiring
2.	perfect	you (pl.) did/made/have done/have made
3.	perfect	I took/have taken
4.	imperfect	we were throwing
5.	present	they want/wish/desire
6.	imperfect	faciebamus
7.	present	capiunt
8.	perfect	iecistis
9.	imperfect	cupiebant
10.	present	iacit

8.2

1.	imperfect	cupiebatis	you (pl.) were wanting/wishing/desiring
2.	present	capimus	we take
3.	perfect	fecerunt	they did/made/ have done/have made
4.	present	iaciunt	they throw
5.	imperfect	capiebamus	we were taking

8.3

1.	imperfect	cupiebam	I was wanting/wishing/desiring
2.	perfect	cepit	he/she/it took/has taken
3.	present	iacis	you (s.) throw
4.	present	cupit	he/she/it wants/wishes/desires
5.	imperfect	iaciebas	you (s.) were throwing

8.4

1.   The messenger took the sword and hurried into battle.
2.   The allies were often throwing spears and arrows.
3.   The famous man always made new shields.
4.   Why do you not want/wish/desire to hear the well-known girl?
5.   We were wanting/wishing/desiring to sail (away) from the savage god immediately.
6.   vinum faciebas.
7.   socii nuntium capiunt.
8.   poeta cantare cupivit.
9.   aurum in caelum iecimus.
10.   agricolam perterritum ceperunt.

8.5

1. Master, watch the/your sons!
2. Run from the town!
3. Slave, enter into the field and lead the horses!/Enter into the field, slave, and lead the horses!
4. Order the slaves of the women to work in the fields!
5. Give the water to the friend immediately!
6. puellae, cibum parate!/cibum, puellae, parate!
7. pueri, statim dormite!
8. ancilla, reginam mone!/reginam, ancilla, mone!
9. filia, equum cape!/equum, filia, cape!
10. filiae, equos capite!/equos, filiae capite!

8.6

1. Many inhabitants were/have been present in the battle.
2. Many sailors were absent from the/their fatherland.
3. You (s.) were/have been absent; therefore the/your slaves were not working.
4. The teacher was shouting to the boys, 'Be good!'
5. However the boys said, 'We wish to be bad.'
6. diu afuerunt.
7. amicus reginae adest.
8. ab oppido aberamus.
9. in agro adesse cupiebatis.
10. magister aberat/afuit.

8.7

1. The messenger of the allies.
2. To the well-known queen.
3. (The strong sailors) often attack the fields and temples.
4. Angry. (work out answer from information that 'The anger of the queen was great')
5. Men; soon. (They were soon present.)
6. Any two from: 'Immediately take the shields and swords!' / 'Hurry to the fatherland of our allies!' / 'Kill the sailors!'

8.8

Therefore the men soon came with the messenger into the fatherland. They watched the sailors for a long time. At last a farmer, who was leading the men, ordered (them), 'Hurry into the waves!' They fought bravely in the waves against the sailors. Soon the sailors were greatly afraid and many sailed from the savage battle across the high waves.

8.9

1.(a) nautarum
1.(b) dic (irregular imperative of dico – 'I say')
2. ablative – the preposition de takes the ablative case
3. clamabat (change from the perfect to the imperfect of clamo, clamare, clamavi, clamatum – 1st conjugation)
4. He/she/it said. If you contradict someone you disagree with them. The English word derives from the Latin words 'contra' = 'against' and 'dico' – 'I say'.
5. perfect, absum
6. templa (accusative neuter plural)
7. magistri ambulare cupiunt. (ambulare = infinitive)
8. agricolae perterriti scuta portabant. (agricolae = masculine, so use a masculine form of the adjective. scuta = accusative neuter plural)

Chapter 9

9.1

1. The inhabitants were terrified when the queen suddenly destroyed the town.
   Note that alternative versions of word order are acceptable. For example 'when the queen suddenly destroyed the town, the inhabitants were terrified'.
2. When your messenger entered into the temple, he greatly praised the Roman goddesses.
3. The maid-servants were wishing to depart from the fields because the sailor was carrying spears and arrows.
4. I decided to write the words of the poet because they were beautiful.
5. The boys, when they were running in the fields, often used to watch the horses of the masters.
6. quod socios timuimus, muros aedificavimus.
7. nautae, ubi ad insulam navigaverunt, fessi erant.
8. incolis, quod amici nostri sunt, auxilium misimus.
9. pueri, quod laeti sunt, in undas currere cupiunt.
10. ubi erat periculum patriae, multos gladios (habere) cupiebatis.

9.2

1.	present	they come
2.	imperfect	we were
3.	perfect	they (have) departed
4.	present imperative	attack! (pl.)
5.	perfect	he/she/it gave/has given
6.	imperfect	oppugnabamus
7.	perfect	navigavi
8.	imperfect	audiebatis
9.	perfect	afuisti
10.	present infinitive	facere

9.3

1.	ablative	from the battle
2.	genitive	of the daughters
3.	accusative	women (object)
4.	vocative	O slave!
5.	accusative	near the temples
6.	ablative	(cum) gladiis
7.	vocative	puellae
8.	dative	incolae
9.	accusative	bella
10.	genitive	viri

9.4

1.	plural genitive masculine	of the sacred sons
2.	plural accusative masculine	the tired inhabitants (object)
3.	plural accusative neuter	to/towards the savage battles
4.	singular vocative feminine	O strong woman
5.	plural ablative feminine	with the good girls
6.	singular accusative masculine	murum altum
7.	plural vocative masculine	o agricolae mali (agricolae is masculine 1st declension)
8.	singular ablative feminine	(cum) magna sagitta
9.	plural genitive masculine	nautarum parvorum (nauta is masculine 1st declension)
10.	plural nominative neuter	oppida pulchra

9.5

1. subito – time
    The crowd of men suddenly attacked our towns.
2. fortiter – manner
    We were fighting bravely in the savage battle with swords.
3. statim – time
    I ordered the tired slaves to carry the books immediately.
4. ibi – place
    There in the sky are great gods.
5. bene – manner
    The ally of the friend spoke well about the war. (amici = gen. s.; socius = nom. s.)
6. where/ubi – place
    ubi sunt filiae malae magistri?
7. often/saepe – time
    muros saepe aedificabamus.
8. greatly/magnopere – manner
    'mane!' clamavi, 'agricolas magnopere times.'
9. soon/mox – time
    mox undas parvas videbamus.
10. once/olim – time
    olim feminae equos dare constituistis.

9.6

1. He was drinking wine and water with his friends.
2. A messenger.
3. A savage monster.
4. It used to live in the waves, but it departed out of the waves and came onto the land.
5. It killed the/some girls.
6. 'Hurry and kill the monster.'

9.7

We heard the man but we did not depart. Then Julius shouted, 'I (shall) fight against the monster!' The farmer said, 'Julius, take my sword,' and (he) gave his sword to Julius. He was running towards the waves and we were also walking with Julius across the fields and near the waves. We stood there, but Julius came towards the monster. He shouted, 'Monster, I (shall) kill you with the help of the gods and the sword of the farmer.'

9.8

1.(a)   monstrum (line 1, final word)
1.(b)   superavi
2.   accusative – it is the object of the sentence
3.   3rd person singular, perfect, iacio
4.   iussi (iubeo, iubere, iussi, iussum = I order)
5.   it turns the sentence into a question
6.   monet (change from the perfect to the present of moneo, monere, monui, monitum – 2nd conjugation)
7.   'gladium' means 'sword'. A gladiator was an ancient Roman fighter who fought against other men to amuse spectators. Gladiators were armed with different weapons, sometimes including swords. Both words are to do with weapons or the people who carry them.
8.   multas ancillas habebas. ('used to' – imperfect)
9.   oppida oppugnavimus. ('oppida' – neuter plural)

Chapter 10

10.1

1 The Greeks took the town (of Troy) and destroyed it.
2 At last. (also accept 'after ten years' – worked out from 'decimos annos Graeci Troiam oppugnabant – the Greeks were attacking Troy for ten years')
3 Wretched men/terrified women.
4 In the streets and (even/also) in the temples.
5 He prepared to depart.
6 His friends. (half mark for 'his' – suis, half mark for 'friends' – amicis)
7 To found a new town in a safe place.

10.2

At last they came to a beautiful land. Suddenly the friends heard men. A great crowd of inhabitants was building walls and temples. Then a man showed Aeneas and his allies to the queen. The queen said, 'Stay and eat food!' And so the friends decided to stay. Dido greatly loved Aeneas but Mercury, the messenger of the gods, said to the man, 'Why do you stay here? Sail to your new fatherland immediately!'

10.3

1.(a) spectate/mittite
1.(b) nuntio (line 1, 2nd word)
2. accusative – the preposition 'trans' takes the accusative
3. currit (change verb from the perfect to the present of curro, currere, cucurri, cursum – 3rd conjugation)
4. 'he/she was fearing.' Timid. If you are timid you often fear things. Both words come from 'timeo' = 'I fear'.
5. 3rd person singular, perfect, capio
6. subject – Dido
   object – gladium (not vinum – it is the object of bibit. The sentence means 'Dido drank the wine, she took the sword and held it.')
7. nautae laeti rident. (the word 'nautae' is 1st declension masculine, therefore requires a masculine form of the adjective)
8. domini cantabant.